CRAB-APPLE

FLOWER·FAIRIES
OF·THE·AUTUMN

This edition first published 1985 by
Blackie and Son Limited
Furnival House · 14–18 High Holborn · London WC1V 6BX

British Library Cataloguing in Publication Data
Barker, Cicely M.
Flower Fairies of the Autumn.
I. Title
821'.912   PR6003.A6786

ISBN 0-216-91690-9

Printed in Great Britain by
Cambus Litho, East Kilbride

FLOWER·FAIRIES OF·THE·AUTUMN

With the nuts and berries they bring

AUTUMN

Poems and pictures by

CICELY MARY BARKER

BLACKIE

THE SONG OF THE
BERRY-QUEEN

An elfin rout,
  With berries laden,
Throngs round about
  A merry maiden.

Red–gold her gown;
  Sun-tanned is she;
She wears a crown
  Of bryony.

The sweet Spring came,
  And lovely Summer:
Guess, then, her name –
  This latest-comer!

SEE ABOVE THE FAIRY'S
HEAD, GUELDER-ROSE'S
BERRIES RED.

THE SONG OF THE
MOUNTAIN ASH FAIRY

They thought me, once, a magic tree
 Of wonderous lucky charm,
And at the door they planted me
 To keep the house from harm.

They have no fear of witchcraft now,
 Yet here am I to-day;
I've hung my berries from the bough,
 And merrily I say:

"Come, all you blackbirds, bring your wives,
 Your sons and daughters too,
The finest banquet of your lives
 Is here prepared for you."

MOUNTAIN ASH

THE SONG OF THE
BLACKBERRY FAIRY

My berries cluster black and thick
For rich and poor alike to pick.

I'll tear your dress, and cling, and tease,
And scratch your hands and arms and
      knees.

I'll stain your fingers and your face,
And then I'll laugh at your disgrace.

But when the bramble-jelly's made,
You'll find your trouble well repaid.

BLACKBERRY

THE SONG OF THE
ROBIN'S PINCUSHION FAIRY

People come and look at me,
Asking who this rogue may be?
—Up to mischief, they suppose,
Perched upon the briar-rose.

I am nothing else at all
But a fuzzy-wuzzy ball,
Like a little bunch of flame;
I will tell you how I came:

First there came a naughty fly,
Pricked the rose, and made her cry;
Out I popped to see about it;
This is true, so do not doubt it!

ROBIN'S PINCUSHION

THE SONG OF THE
ELDERBERRY FAIRY

Tread quietly:
O people, hush!
—For don't you see
A spotted thrush,
One thrush or two,
Or even three,
In every laden elder-tree?

They pull and lug,
They flap and push,
They peck and tug
To strip the bush;
They have forsaken
Snail and slug;
Unseen I watch them, safe and snug!

ELDERBERRY

THE SONG OF THE
ACORN FAIRY

To English folk the mighty oak
   Is England's noblest tree;
Its hard-grained wood is strong and good
   As English hearts can be.
And would you know how oak-trees grow,
   The secret may be told:
You do but need to plant for seed
   One acorn in the mould;
For even so, long years ago,
   Were born the oaks of old.

ACORN

THE SONG OF THE
DOGWOOD FAIRY

I was a warrior,
  When, long ago,
Arrows of Dogwood
  Flew from the bow.
Passers-by, nowadays,
  Go up and down,
Not one remembering
  My old renown.
Yet when the Autumn sun
  Colours the trees,
Should you come seeking me,
  Know me by these:
Bronze leaves and crimson leaves,
  Soon to be shed;
Dark little berries,
  On stalks turning red.

DOGWOOD

THE SONG OF THE
PRIVET FAIRY

Here in the wayside hedge I stand,
And look across the open land;
Rejoicing thus, unclipped and free,
I think how you must envy me,
O garden Privet, prim and neat,
With tidy gravel at your feet!

PRIVET

THE SONG OF THE
HORSE CHESTNUT FAIRY

My conkers, they are shiny things,
  And things of mighty joy,
And they are like the wealth of kings
  To every little boy;
I see the upturned face of each
  Who stands around the tree:
He sees his treasure out of reach,
  But does not notice *me*.

For love of conkers bright and brown,
  He pelts the tree all day;
With stones and sticks he knocks them down,
  And thinks it jolly play.
But sometimes I, the elf, am hit
  Until I'm black and blue:
O laddies, only wait a bit,
  I'll shake them down to you!

HORSE CHESTNUT

THE SONG OF THE
SLOE FAIRY

When Blackthorn blossoms leap to sight,
They deck the hedge with starry light,
    In early Spring
    When rough winds blow,
    Each promising
    A purple sloe.

And now is Autumn here, and lo,
The Blackthorn bears the purple sloe!
      But ah, how much
      Too sharp these plums,
      Until the touch
      Of Winter comes!

SLOE

THE SONG OF THE
NIGHTSHADE BERRY FAIRY

"You see my berries, how they gleam and
    glow,
Clear ruby-red, and green, and orange-
    yellow;
Do they not tempt you, fairies, dangling so?"
   The fairies shake their heads and answer "No!
    You are a crafty fellow!"

"What, won't you try them? There is
    naught to pay!
Why should you think my berries poisoned
    things?
You fairies may look scared and fly away—
The children will believe me when I say
    My fruit is for kings!"
  But all good fairies cry in anxious haste,
"O children, do not taste!"

NIGHTSHADE BERRY

THE SONG OF THE
BLACK BRYONY FAIRY

Bright and wild and beautiful
For the Autumn festival,
I will hang from tree to tree
Wreaths and ropes of Bryony,
To the glory and the praise
Of the sweet September days.

BLACK BRYONY

THE SONG OF THE
WHITE BRYONY FAIRY

Have you seen at Autumn-time
    Fairy-folk adorning
All the hedge with necklaces,
    Early in the morning?
Green beads and red beads
    Threaded on a vine:
Is there any handiwork
    Prettier than mine?

WHITE BRYONY

THE SONG OF THE
HAZEL-NUT FAIRY

Slowly, slowly, growing
    While I watched them well,
See, my nuts have ripened;
    Now I've news to tell.
I will tell the Squirrel,
    "Here's a store for you;
But, kind Sir, remember
    The Nuthatch likes them too."

I will tell the Nuthatch,
    "Now, Sir, you may come;
Choose your nuts and crack them,
    But leave the children some."
I will tell the children,
    "You may take your share;
Come and fill your pockets,
    But leave a few to spare."

HAZEL-NUT

THE SONG OF THE
WAYFARING TREE FAIRY

My shoots are tipped with buds as dusty-grey
As ancient pilgrims toiling on their way.

Like Thursday's child with far to go, I stand,
All ready for the road to Fairyland;

With hood, and bag, and shoes, my name to suit,
And in my hand my gorgeous-tinted fruit.

WAYFARING TREE

THE SONG OF THE
HAWTHORN FAIRY

These thorny branches bore the May
　　So many months ago,
That when the scattered petals lay
　　Like drifts of fallen snow,
"This is the story's end," you said;
　　But O, not half was told!
For see, my haws are here instead,
And hungry birdies shall be fed
　　On these when days are cold.

HAWTHORN

THE SONG OF THE
ROSE HIP FAIRY

Cool dewy morning,
　　Blue sky at noon,
White mist at evening,
　　And large yellow moon;

Blackberries juicy
　　For staining of lips;
And scarlet, O scarlet
　　The Wild Rose Hips!

Gay as a gipsy
　　All Autumn long,
Here on the hedge-top
　　This is my song.

ROSE HIP

THE SONG OF THE
BEECHNUT FAIRY

O the great and happy Beech,
    Glorious and tall!
Changing with the changing months,
    Lovely in them all:

Lovely in the leafless time,
    Lovelier in green;
Loveliest with golden leaves
    And the sky between,

When the nuts are falling fast,
    Thrown by little me—
Tiny things to patter down
    From a forest tree!

BEECHNUT

THE SONG OF THE
CRAB-APPLE FAIRY

Crab-apples, Crab-apples, out in the wood,
Little and bitter, yet little and good!
The apples in orchards, so rosy and fine,
Are children of wild little apples like mine.

The branches are laden, and droop to the
    ground;
The fairy-fruit falls in a circle around;
Now all you good children, come gather them up;
They'll make you sweet jelly to spread when
    you sup.

One little apple I'll catch for myself;
I'll stew it, and strain it, to store on a shelf
In four or five acorn-cups, locked with a key
In a cupboard of mine at the root of the tree.